Lion Roars

BE BOLD!

PARENT TIPS

Be Bold! books are designed to engage little listeners, introduce them to young animals, and demonstrate positive behaviors and values.

This story shows a lion cub's introduction to pride members. It must learn quickly how to navigate new relationships with both adults and older cubs. Finding its voice helps a cub assimilate into a larger group, a crucial step that ensures its very survival.

When a child meets new people and feels shy or unsure, you might help them find commonalities—the seeds from which friendships grow—as well as teach them the importance of finding their voice. Both are necessary parts of navigating relationships successfully and moving a step closer to becoming well-rounded, confident individuals.

As I get bigger, I play in the sunshine with my brothers and sisters.

We sneak and chase. Pounce and WRESTLE!

Mama calls me close.

I try to copy her roars.

We meet aunties and cousins. They growl hellos.

One bossy cousin bites my ear. Ow!

I try to roar for her to STOP. Not quite loud ENOUGH ...

We learn new games.

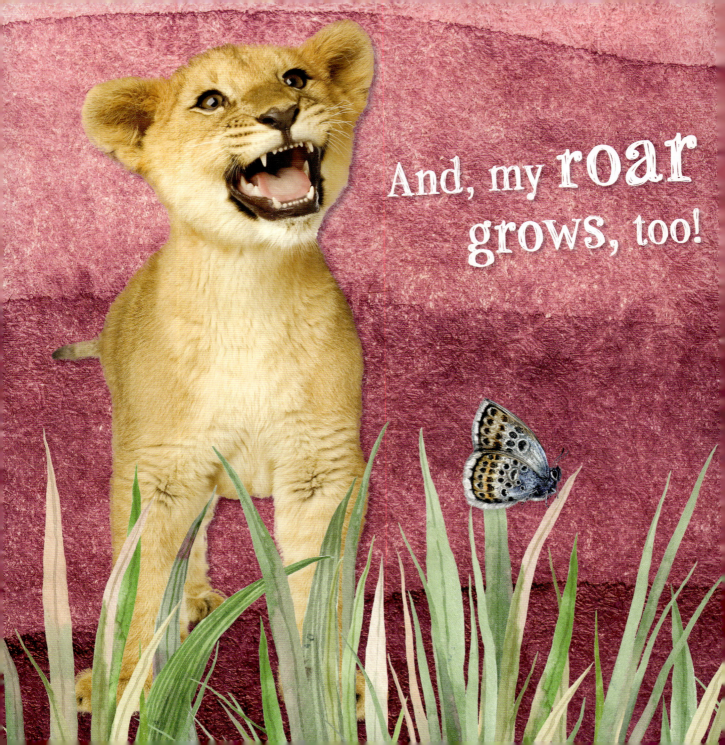

mew-rowwr.

MROWWR!

Someday, watch out!
I will be as big and fierce
as Papa and Mama.